Japan

Zoë Dawson

RSVP ®

RAINTREE
STECK-VAUGHN
PUBLISHERS
The Steck-Vaughn Company

Austin, Texas

Published by Raintree Steck-Vaughn Publishers, an imprint of Steck-Vaughn Company

A ZOË BOOK

Editor: Kath Davies, Helene Resky
Design: Jan Sterling, Sterling Associates
Map: Gecko Limited
Production: Grahame Griffiths

Library of Congress Cataloging-in-Publication Data

Dawson, Zoë.
    Japan / Zoë Dawson.
        p. cm. — (Postcards from)
    Includes index.
    ISBN 0-8172-4011-X (lib. binding)
    ISBN 0-8172-4232-5 (softcover)
        1. Japan — Description and travel — Juvenile literature.
    [1. Japan — Description and travel. 2. Letters.]
    I. Title. II. Series.
    DS811.S44 1996
    952–dc20   95–10035
                                                              CIP
                                                              AC
Printed and bound in the United States
1 2 3 4 5 6 7 8 9 0 WZ 99 98 97 96 95

Photographic acknowledgments

The publishers wish to acknowledge, with thanks, the following photographic sources:

The Hutchison Library / Michael MacIntyre - cover bl, 6, 14, 26; / Liba Taylor 8; / Jon Burbank 10; Robert Harding Picture Library / Gavin Hellier - title page, 20; Zefa - cover tl & r, 12, 16, 18, 22, 24, 28.

The publishers have made every effort to trace the copyright holders, but if they have inadvertently overlooked any, they will be pleased to make the necessary arrangement at the first opportunity.

Contents

All the words that appear in **bold** are explained in the Glossary on page 30.

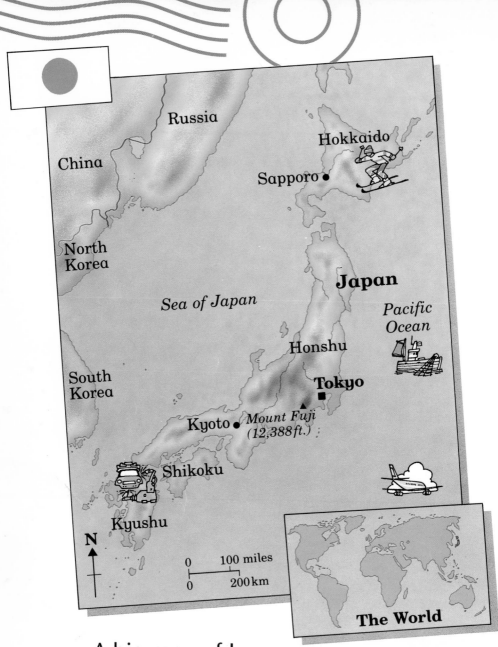

A big map of Japan
and a small map of the world

4

Dear Kim,

Japan is a long way from home. You can see Japan in red on the small map. We are on Honshu. It is the biggest island in Japan. Lots of people live here. Can you find Honshu on the big map?

Love,

Pat

P.S. Mom says that Japan is much smaller than the United States. It is made up of about 4,000 islands. More than 100 million people live here.

A street in the middle of Tokyo

Dear Tom,

It took about 12 hours to fly from Los Angeles to Tokyo. Most people in Japan do not speak English. They speak only Japanese. Japanese writing looks like pictures.

Your friend,

Daniel

P.S. Dad says that nearly a quarter of all the people in Japan live in or around Tokyo. It is the **capital** city of Japan.

Choosing a present from a store in Tokyo

Dear Katie,

Japanese money is called *yen*. Mom gave me some *yen* to buy presents. Japanese people buy lots of presents. People in the stores pack each present in a pretty paper box.

Love,

Jenny

P.S. Mom says that Japanese people are very polite. They bring small presents with them every time they visit friends. This is a way of saying "thank you."

A plate of salad and raw fish, called *sashimi*

Dear Joanne,

Japanese people like to eat fresh food. They eat a lot of fish. People eat their food with **chopsticks**. They do not use knives and forks, but they do use spoons.

Love,

Teddy

P.S. Some **restaurants** show different dishes in the window. You can see what is in each dish. You choose the ones you want to eat before you go inside.

The "bullet train" passing Mount Fuji

Dear Juanita,

We saw Mount Fuji today. It is the highest mountain in Japan. We also went on the "bullet train." It is the fastest train in Japan. It travels at more than 150 miles an hour (240 kph).

Love,

José

P.S. Dad says that many people travel by train in Japan because the roads are so crowded. In many cities the railroad lines run under the ground.

A farm and rice fields near Kyoto

Dear Sue,

Most of the farms in Japan are very small. Many farmers use machines in the fields. Some people do the work by hand. They grow a lot of rice and some fruit and vegetables.

Love,

Anna

P.S. Mom says that most people in Japan eat rice at every meal. Some Japanese people like the food we eat for breakfast. We have the same kind of breakfast here as we do at home.

Inside a Japanese house

Dear Jon,

Most people here live in new apartment **complexes**. Old houses are made of wood. The walls inside are made of paper. People sit on mats or **cushions** on the floor.

Love,

Kelly

P.S. Mom says that Japanese people take their shoes off when they go into a house. They leave their shoes in the hall.

A crowded beach in summer

Dear Maria,

It is very hot in Japan during the summer. Children have school vacation for six weeks. Lots of people go to the beach. Some people travel by boat from one island to another.

Love,

Carl

P.S. Dad says that it is cooler in the spring. Lots of people go to the country to see the cherry blossoms.

A special house made of snow at Sapporo, on Hokkaido island

Dear Joe,

It is cold in Japan during the winter. Special houses are made out of snow for the **festival** in Sapporo. People go skiing in the mountains on Honshu island on weekends.

Your friend,

Ben

P.S. Mom says that there are hot water springs in the mountains. Some people go to soak in them, even in the winter.

The Shinto gate at Kyoto

Dear Jo,

This big red gate is called a *torii*. There are lots of them in Japan. A *torii* is a gate to a special place. People who follow the **Shinto** religion go to these special places to pray.

Love,

Mary

P.S. Mom says that most Japanese people visit a Shinto **shrine**. They go to a shrine to pray for good luck.

May 5th is Children's Day in Japan. Many
children dress up for this special day.

Dear Gina,

We have not seen many Japanese children around. They are at school every day except Sunday. Sometimes girls dress up like this on special days. They wear long dresses called *kimonos*.

Love,

Lori

P.S. Sometimes Japanese families dress up to visit a shrine. Dad says that they pray for the children to do well at school.

The "crane dance" at Yasaka shrine
in Kyoto

Dear Tia,

We went to a festival in Kyoto. The people who danced wore special clothes. Some of the **headdresses** were made of paper. The music was different from any I have heard before.

Love,

Sanjit

P.S. Dad says that Kyoto was the capital city of Japan for hundreds of years. The rulers were called **emperors** and **empresses**. They lived in Kyoto.

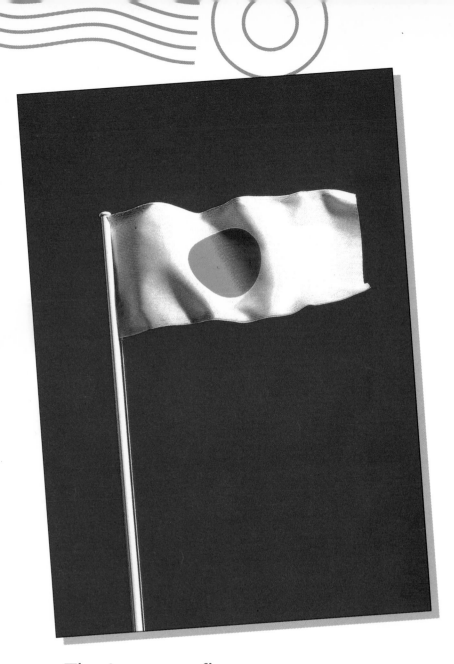

The Japanese flag

Dear Suzie,

The Japanese name for Japan is Nippon. This means "the land of the rising sun." The red circle on the Japanese flag stands for the sun.

Love,

Lisa

P.S. Mom says that long ago the people believed that the emperor was the sun god. Now the people choose their leaders, and the emperor does not rule. Japan is a **democracy**.

Glossary

Capital: The town or city where people who rule the country meet. The capital is not always the biggest city in the country.

Chopsticks: Two long sticks that are used for eating food. Both chopsticks are held between the fingers of one hand.

Complexes: Group of buildings

Cushion: A soft pillow or pad

Democracy: A country where the people choose the leaders they want to run the country

Emperor: A man who rules several different lands or kingdoms

Empress: A woman who rules several different lands or kingdoms

Festival: A time when people celebrate something special or a special time of year

Headdress: A fancy covering for the head

P.S.: This stands for Post Script which means "to write after." A postscript is the part of a card or letter that is added at the end, after the person has signed it.

Restaurant: A place where people go to eat meals. They pay for the food they eat.

Shinto: A Japanese religion in which everything in nature has its own god

Shrine: A special place or a building where people go to pray

Index

beaches 18–19
boats 19

children 19, 24, 25
chopsticks 11
cities 7, 13, 27

dancing 26–27

families 25
farms 14–15
festivals 21, 27
food 10–11, 15

Hokkaido 20
Honshu 5, 21
houses 16–17, 20, 21

islands 5, 19, 20, 21

kimonos 25
Kyoto 14, 22, 26, 27

money 9
mountains 13, 21
music 27

religion 23
roads 13
rulers 27, 29

Sapporo 20, 21
school 25
Shinto 22, 23
skiing 21
spring 19
stores 8, 9
summer 18–19

Tokyo 6–7, 8
trains 12, 13

vacations 19

winter 21
writing 7

DATE DUE

GAYLORD			PRINTED IN U.S.A